Red Hot Chili Peppers

A rare insight through the eyes of band photographer Tony Woolliscroft

Me and my friends

Foreword by Chad Smith

Abrams Image
New York

TONY AND I JOINED THE PEPPERS AT ABOUT THE SAME TIME...

On my first tour of Europe in the cold ass winter of 1990, we headed off to England. I was so excited to be in a country that spawned so many of my musical idols: Sabbath, Zeppelin, The Who, Deep Purple, Queen, etc. This is the music I grew up on and I couldn't believe I was over here in their backyards. Needless to say I was a little green and, being the 'new guy', I was on my own a lot. I remember meeting Tony, this big cuddly bear, and he came up to me at his first photo shoot with us for Kerrang, I think, and asked me where the "loo" was and I couldn't understand a fucking word he said, except for maybe that one. And I didn't know anybody named Lou. Mind you I hadn't been in England too long and his accent, being a northern one, was as thick as a brick. "Funniest guy yet," I thought. Anyway, from that day forward, he has shot us on every one of our tours all over the world. Every one. All of them... Jesus, stay home once in a while!

Now, along the way our little combo has gotten better and more popular, and Tony's photos have been published in every format imaginable. I always know when we show up to play, I will get that bear hug and a "howya doin' matey?" and I don't even have to turn around to know who it is. Most photographers are only allowed to shoot the first three songs of a show. We love Tony and his work so much that he is the only guy we give complete access to for an entire show. That's how much we trust him.

But you'll be able to see that trust going through this book. His images make you feel like you're there. Like any true artist, and much like our band, he keeps searching and trying to learn more about his craft. He has grown with us. I think you will see that growth here as well. He has captured the essence of our band on film. Some of these shots have come to be through various publications that sent Tony to shoot us. But other shots have been generated by Tony just coming out on tour for the love of the music. Magazines and record companies don't like to pay too much. So Tony will pay his own way so as not to miss an important gig. He might have even slept on my hotel room couch once or twice.

I'm sure he would like nothing better than to be kickin' it on the Anfield pitch, rooting on his beloved Liverpool footballers, than be trying to get a shot of a grumpy band going on stage in Venezuela or Chicago... or Woodstock – both times.

He has been at all our most memorable shows... like John's first show with us in Washington D.C. after he rejoined the band in 1998. It was the Free Tibet show at JFK stadium, and we were nervous to go on after lightning struck a girl in the audience the day before. We huddled backstage right before we were about to go on, using borrowed equipment from Pearl Jam. Usually we hold hands and say a little something to each other, but this time we hugged and supported each other. It was a new beginning. That picture is on the back of our Californication booklet. Tony captured that moment like nobody else could. You also might see a page of me flipping off the camera... I don't know why that started, but Tony was the catalyst. But now we always laugh when he tries to sneak up on me, 'cause he knows the finger is coming!

Easy going and fun to be around, he's been with us through thick and thin. I recall coming off stage at one of our biggest gigs in Ireland and he stopped me with a sincere look of love in his eyes to tell me how proud he was of us. That meant a lot.

I hope you see his passion for his art, for music and for people. We're still growing with him, letting him capture the good times and bad times, happy and sad. But what we are most proud of is that he captures the love.

Chad Smith, Drummer, Red Hot Chili Peppers

"We huddled backstage right before we were about to go on, using borrowed equipment from Pearl Jam. Usually we hold hands and say a little something to each other, but this time we hugged and supported each other. It was a new beginning..."

Library of Congress Cataloging-in-Publication Data

Woolliscroft, Tony.
Red Hot Chili Peppers / photographs by Tony Woolliscroft ;
contribution by Chad Smith.
        p. cm.
Includes bibliographical references and index.
ISBN 978-0-8109-8283-3 (alk. paper)
1. Red Hot Chili Peppers (Musical group)—Pictorial works.
2. Rock groups—United States—Pictorial works. I. Smith, Chad, 1962- II. Title.

ML421.R4W66 2009
782.42166092'2—dc22
2009009441

First UK edition published by Trinity Mirror, 2008.

Published in 2009 by Abrams Image, an imprint of ABRAMS.

Printed and bound in China
10 9 8 7 6 5 4 3 2 1

Abrams Image books are available at special discounts when purchased in
quantity for premiums and promotions as well as fundraising or educational use.
Special editions can also be created to specification. For details, contact
specialmarkets@abramsbooks.com or the address below.

115 West 18th Street
New York, NY 10011
www.abramsbooks.com

INTRODUCTION: TONY WOOLLISCROFT

I'm sitting in the back room of my home and every inch of the floor is covered with Red Hot Chili Peppers pictures. I'm going slightly insane looking at them all. It's then I realise just how many pictures I have actually taken of the band over the years and all the places I've seen them. What I've tried to do in this book is share some very memorable times I've had photographing them. I called it 'Me and My Friends' simply because it was one of my favourite songs by the band. I do class them as friends, and I don't think I would have been allowed as near to them if they didn't class me as one. They are very private people. Photographically, I got as close to them as you could.

A few years ago a leading magazine described this band as 'indestructible'. This is the most apt headline I think anybody had ever come up with for them. Why? Because I think it's true. It's been a mad rollercoaster ride shooting them for the best part of 20 years, let me tell you. There have been times when I thought it had gone, it was over, but there was an amazing will to keep this band going that I can only look upon with admiration. The setbacks these guys have gone through, most people would have called it a day, wondered if it was all worth it. Not these guys. They wanted to reach the top, to be the best, both of which they have done, in my eyes.

I first heard the band in one of my best friend's flat in Bradford. His name was Rob Heaton and he was the drummer in New Model Army, who happened to be on the same UK label as the Peppers, EMI. Rob had got hold of the new Peppers cd 'Uplift Mofo Party Plan'. I was taken aback at how good it was and how different it sounded to what I was listening to at that time. I wanted to see this band. Rob's wife, Robin, was from Orange County, California, the band's home state. She raved about them, saying how good they were live. The first RHCP hooks had landed in my skin. I missed them on the 'Uplift' tour, something I still regret to this day. So when Mother's Milk came out I made damn sure I saw them.

I've been a very lucky man really. I've travelled the world taking pictures of bands for a living. Very early on in my career I was asked by Raw magazine to shoot the Peppers live. I jumped at the chance. I had badgered them into submission to give me work after another best friend in the world, Craig Duffy, got my foot in the door there. If I'm truthful, I was a good live photographer then, but that was about it. I could capture action very well. It was the thing that got me through in those days, plus I had a good basic understanding of a camera thanks to my dad giving me his old 35mm Kodak when he got a new SLR. This helped me a lot in my early days.

When I first saw the Peppers I was mesmerised, I really was. I'd been going to gigs since I was 13 years old, hundreds of them up and down the UK and across Europe following bands. I'd seen nothing like these guys. Sparks seemed to fly off stage between each band member. Their workrate was phenomenal. Nonstop. The energy, God, it was infectious. They played harder and heavier than Metallica and Slayer put together. It was an exciting time in the late '80s, early 90's. There was a wave of great new music coming out of the West Coast of the USA and the Peppers were one of these bands at the forefront. It was a great time for me taking pictures. I hated all those LA hair bands. I grew up on Punk, so bands like the Peppers, Jane's Addiction and Faith No More, I immediately loved. As a consequence I beat Raw over the head every time the Peppers came back to the UK to do something with them. They got sick of me going on about them.

I'm sure the band used to think, who the bloody hell is this showing up at our gigs all the time taking pictures. I got friendly with the crew at the time, Mark Johnson and Robbie Allen. They became good friends. Then they got a new Tour Manager, Tony Selinger, a great guy who I met on the road a few times. This got me close to the band. I finally started speaking to Anthony and Chad and got on great with both of them. This is where it all started I think. AK put me in touch with Lindy Goetz at LGM, the band's management, even though he must have been thinking "who is this mad English guy who wants to come to the US to shoot the band?"

Give all of these people their due, they welcomed me with open arms. No one thought I was trying to make a quick buck selling my pictures, as I got closer to them. I think they were moved a little, as my timing was usually rubbish trying to get a trip out of the record companies to cover the gigs. I funded virtually everything myself until Woodstock in 1999. That was nearly 10 years! I just wanted to go and shoot the band. I liked them so much.

With the book, I've tried to give you an insight into my little world shooting the Peppers through the years. I could easily have filled it 20 times over just with pictures of Anthony, Flea, Chad and John. But that's not the whole story and that's what makes their story so special, so, you will find pictures of Dave Navarro and Arik Marshall as they are part of my story with the band. As well as the thousands I've tortuously had to leave out, there are a few pictures missing from my collection, like a very early session shot with the band before they went on stage in San Francisco. In those days, shooting on slide film, there was only one copy. They get scattered across magazines around the world, then you struggle to get them back.

I have shared many amazing moments shooting this band, seeing the dayGlo effect of that outstanding UV show at the Astoria in London, trying to take pictures of them playing in a typhoon in Japan, watching an amazing comeback show with John in Washington RFK stadium, capturing AK as he sang Venice Queen, with me locked in that small makeshift studio in the Chateau Marmont hotel in Hollywood (thank you AK it was amazing!), and one of my pictures was used on a certain cd sleeve that sold some, bloody hell, 15,000,000 copies. Wow, that's just a taste...

Hopefully you will see through the pages in this book how my photography grew with the band. I learnt a lot shooting these guys. From the very small venues to the massive stadiums they ended up in, I've met some amazing people along the way, but best of all I got to work with the best band on the planet, bar none.

Hope you enjoy the ride...   *Tony Woolliscroft*

ACKNOWLEDGEMENTS

RHCP: Anthony, Flea, Chad and John

Mum and Dad (for their love and support)

Steve Hanrahan and Rick Cooke (for their vision on this book)

Craig Duffy (for my foot in the door)

Lindy Goetz, Louis Mathieu, Tony Selinger, Terry and Sarah Wells, Dave Lee, Scott Holthaus, Dave Rat, Chris Warren, Blackie, Bill Rahmy, Chris Kansy, Lisa Bloom, Robbie Allen, Mark Ironman Johnson, Mark Petracca, Q prime (Gayle Fine), John Curd, Rob and Robin Heaton, Angela Duffy, Pheobe Sinclair, Dave Navarro, Grier Govorko, Tracey Robar, Bob and Emma, Gag and Sarah, Greeb and Nicky, Vicky Jones, Yemma (Gemma) and Bec (Book title), Titan and Garf.

I could have kept going for ever on this list, so to anybody I have missed personally and professionally, many, many thanks!

Also LIVERPOOL FC for Istanbul and the best night of my life.

CONTENTS

MOTHER'S MILK
GREAT EXPECTATIONS TOUR 1990

FIRST IMPRESSIONS. THE UV LEGEND.
KEEPING ANTHONY IN THE PICTURE

The first time I saw the Chili Peppers play I was blown away but I cursed myself for not having my cameras with me. The band came to Europe in January 1990 to promote their latest album, Mother's Milk. It was John Frusciante and Chad Smith's first tour of Europe as the two new members of the band. The night before the London show, myself and Craig Duffy (one of my best friends), who worked for the promoter of the gig, John Curd, drove to Portsmouth University to see the band and touch base with the crew and tour manager.

We arrived just as the band came on stage. It was utter chaos from the first note but was absolutely amazing. It was packed to the rafters, there were kids stage-diving and the band were performing like mad men. I couldn't believe I'd left my cameras back at Craig's flat. My luck changed though when I made contact with the band and crew. We hit it off, and I got given an access-all-areas pass for the rest of the European tour.

The following night at the London Astoria show I arrived with my cameras in hand and shot the whole show. Nelson Mandela had just been released from prison and the band welcomed his freedom and dedicated a song to him. Once again I was blown away by their performance and captured some great live shots.

Chad flips me the finger for the very first time . . .

Included in some of the shots was saxophonist, Tree, who toured with them at the time, but I never saw him play with the band again after these European dates.

The Chilis departed for the rest of the tour but another London show was hastily arranged for the band to play as a last date on their way home, again at the Astoria Theatre. It sold out in minutes. Higher Ground had been released as a single by the record company and had charted in the singles charts. The band were becoming big news in the UK. The show, for those lucky enough to say that they witnessed it, has legendary status. Everybody raved about it for weeks.

When I arrived, the band and crew were busy painting their back-line equipment and anything else in view completely in Ultra-Violet multi-coloured paint. To complete proceedings a huge black paper backdrop was given the full treatment, with the stage bathed completely in UV light, giving it an amazing, colourful 3D effect.

The band retired to the dressing room for their pre-gig rituals and painted themselves from head to toe in the UV paint. Meanwhile, I ran out of the venue and straight down Oxford Street to the nearest photographic shop to get the fastest slide film I could buy, knowing this was the best way to capture the show in its truest form. I got some great shots, but the UV effect began to wear off after about five songs into the set. As the band played harder, the more they sweated...!

A few months later the band came back to the UK for a few more shows, playing Nottingham Rock City and Manchester Apollo. Backstage at Rock City I was showing Anthony and John some of my pictures when Anthony asked if he could borrow my UV shots to take home and get some blown up, including one for his dad, Blackie. They were my only copies at the time, but I lent them to him and he also gave me his home address and phone number to send some more stuff out to him. He was really genuine and it was the beginning of a mutual trust.

A colourful performance
from the guys covered from
head to toe in UV paint

Above and top right: Flea and Chad in the zone
Right: John flexes his guitar muscles
Below: A bit of sax and then Tree was off...

SAN FRANCISCO CIVIC AUDITORIUM, NEW YEAR'S EVE 1990
FLEA TRUMPETS IN THE NEW YEAR. DRINKS AT THE PHOENIX

I tried to get some money out of EMI for this trip. I felt I'd earned the record company quite a lot of publicity for the band that year without them helping to pay for anything. My timing was rubbish. The Chilis had just announced that they were leaving EMI and signing a big deal with Warner Bros. Regardless, me and my friend, Mole, flew out to San Fran on December 28 and stayed with Les and Larry from the band Primus who were kind enough to put us up. They were also playing a couple of their own shows before New Year's Eve and so we went to see them - which was a bonus!

At that time, Mother's Milk was the Chili Peppers' biggest selling album. The New Year's Eve show was one of the last on that worldwide tour. At that point in the US a small number of 'Alternative' bands were beginning to break into the mainstream USA market, the Chili Peppers being one of the bands that helped pave the way for them.

When we arrived at the concert venue on Market Street on the day I was quite shocked by the size of it. The auditorium had a capacity of 10,000 and was quite a step up from the Astoria in London, which held 3,000, the biggest I had seen them play at that point. It gave me a handle on how hard the band had worked on tour in the USA in the years prior to this and it was the first time I'd seen the band play in the US. Again, I was given all-areas passes and a free run to shoot as much as I wanted. Backstage I was introduced to Rick Rubin prior to the band going on stage as he and Flea sat talking. It was hinted that Rick would be producing the band's next album later in 1991.

A very hasty shoot was arranged before the band walked on stage… I sprinted around to the photo pit for the opening bars of 'Out in LA', which at that point was the band's opening song for as long as anyone could remember. Another great show was witnessed, Flea and John playing in multi-coloured oversized dinosaur boots

for the duration. The band stopped at midnight and Flea played Auld Lang Syne on his trumpet while balloons were dropped onto the crowd from the ceiling, everybody wishing each other Happy New Year. The band then carried on with their set. It was a great way to see in the New Year. After the show we all retired to the infamous Phoenix Hotel on Eddy Street for a drink or two and it was about 3am before we all crashed out!

The day after we drove from San Fran to LA with the crew and equipment and a few days later I met up with Anthony in LGM's management offices before I flew home. We had a chat and he safely returned my UV show slides and thanked me for letting him borrow them. He told me to keep in touch as he drove off in his black '67 RS Camaro with the roof down in the winter LA sun.

Far left: Chad plays the drums and my camera at the same time, almost cracking the fish eye lens
Left: Another day at the office for Flea in his giant dinosaur boots and nappy
Below: Balloons drop as the clock strikes midnight
Bottom: Rockin' in the New Year

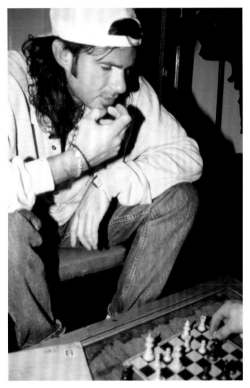

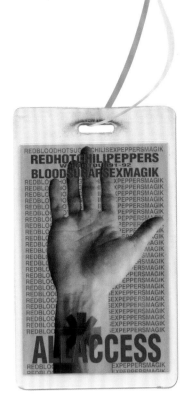

BLOOD SUGAR SEX MAGIK
UK TOUR 1992

THE LONELINESS OF JOHN FRUSCIANTE

This time the European tour had started in Amsterdam, Holland, worked its way all around Europe, and was now on its final leg in the UK. Reports had been sketchy on how good the gigs were. I'd heard through the grapevine that things were not great within the band, but I took no notice. I was looking forward to seeing them and the album had been critically acclaimed by all the music press in the UK.

The opening night on the UK tour was at the Hummingbird in Birmingham. The gig was packed to the rafters and it was incredibly hot in there. From the first note you could tell things weren't quite right in the Chili Peppers camp. John seemed very detached on stage from the rest of the band. The gig wasn't terrible, it just didn't have that great spark that the band always seemed to have and that I was used to seeing from them.

After the show I went upstairs to see the band and say hello. Chad gave me a big hug and asked how I was doing. Anthony looked shattered, and was sat in a chair. He was quite poorly with a bad chest infection. John had already left and Flea was somewhere else. I said I'd see them the following night in Liverpool at the Royal Court Theatre.

The gig was more of the same. I couldn't quite believe it. At the coming show in London I had been asked to take shots for the feature that Raw magazine was running. They wanted dressing room pictures but the session was turned down to keep the peace within the band. The vibe in the dressing room wasn't right. John cut a lonely figure and was keeping himself to himself. Raw journalist Liz Evans sensed this and the magazine ran with the headline 'The Chili Peppers' last (hand) stand' with the main picture of AK pulling a handstand on stage.

Actually, the first of the two nights at London's Brixton Academy was the best show I witnessed on the UK tour, and everybody held hope that the band would weather the storm and come through their difficulties. I couldn't see them the following night as I was given another assignment by Raw.

It would be six years before I would see John Frusciante again. He left the band just after the UK tour, in Japan.

*Top: Nice jacket... Seal backstage
at Brixton with Anthony
Middle: Chad the chess champion
Left: In full flight at the Hummingbird
Far left: John in introspective mood*

TORHOUT AND WERCHTER FESTIVALS, BELGIUM
ARIK MARSHALL'S FIRST GIGS. BRYAN ADAMS MUD-SLINGING

As the tour bus came to collect us I was not looking forward to a concert outdoors. Anthony had me entertaining the band, crew and his guests by getting me to talk in my Northern accent and seeing if anybody on the bus understood what the hell I just said. This kept everybody in stitches for a good half an hour to the festival site. Arik Marshall never said much on the trip, he kept himself to himself. He had only just joined the band after auditions in his native Los Angeles, and was a bit of an unknown.

As we pulled on to the festival site it was quite apparent how hard it had been raining that week. Everybody was covered head to toe in mud. It was like a scene from Apocalypse Now. Bryan Adams was headlining the bill,

with the Chili Peppers as 'Special Guests' next to the headline spot. Also on were Urban Dance Squad and a band hotly tipped to be the next big thing, the Smashing Pumpkins.

It was soon show time. I had been in the photo pit at the front of the stage but found the stage way too high to get decent shots. You could only see the head and shoulders of each band member, so after one song I went back up to the stage and shot the band from there.

I watched Arik closely. It was certainly a baptism of fire for him in front of 50,000 Belgian fans that were covered in mud. He could certainly play. He was note perfect. The only thing missing was that he was not that dynamic on

stage. I was always used to seeing a really lively performance from the band, with a lot of interaction between each member. Arik was very static and tended to concentrate on playing perfectly but not moving from his side of the stage. The band went down great though. In fact a little too great. As soon as it was apparent that they were not coming back on after their last song the crowd started to pelt the stage with mud. Not just a bit of mud, it absolutely rained with the stuff for a good five minutes. The stage was covered, including all of the Chili Peppers' equipment, and Bryan Adams' band equipment. The Adams crew looked on in horror as it happened.

It took an hour and a half to clear the stage and finally get Bryan on an hour late. They didn't look happy...

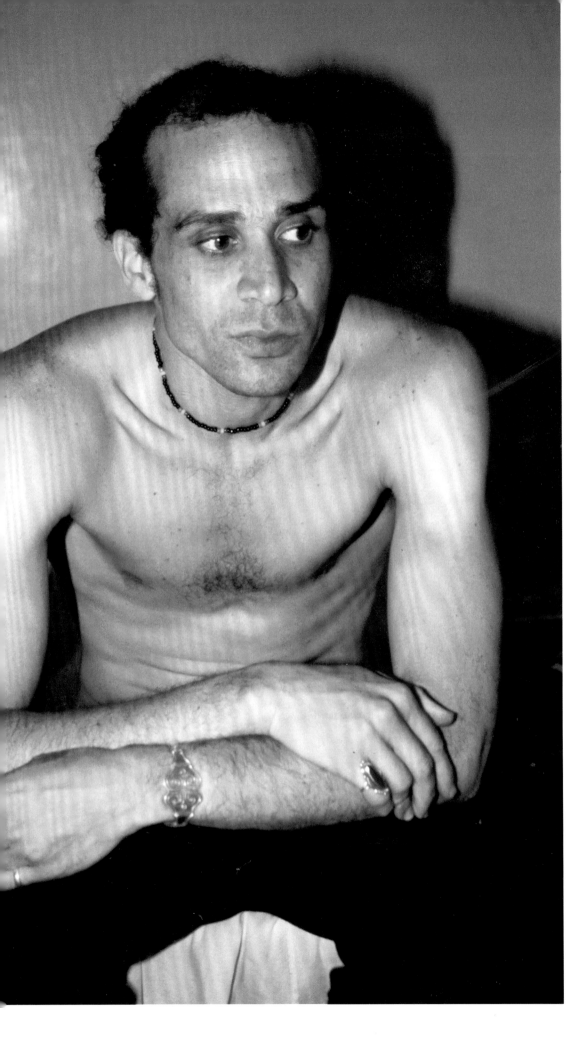

Backstage things were pretty relaxed with the Peppers. I took AK's picture with Henky Penky, a tattooist from Amsterdam, who had done most of the work on his body. The band seemed happy with the first show with Arik. We all ate steak backstage for dinner before climbing on to the bus back to Ostend and the hotel.

The bus collected us next morning and everybody was relieved to see that at least it had stopped raining in Ostend. Unfortunately this wasn't the case in Werchter. Another quagmire awaited.

The day before I had struggled out front to get any decent pictures as the stage was so high, so it was arranged that I would be able to go out to the very front of the stage to get some better shots for two songs while the band played. It was another good performance, with Arik easing in to his job better.

At the end of their set a few bits of mud were thrown up on stage before the crowd got them back for an encore. As Flea walked on, for a joke, he gave the crowd something to aim for by baring his backside. It rained mud and at one point Arik was hiding behind his own guitar amp to take shelter from the onslaught. The Bryan Adams crew again looked less than impressed as the stage and all their equipment was quickly covered in the stuff.

We took the drive back to Ostend and Chad told me of the plan to release 'Under the Bridge' as their next single in the USA. Little did he know then, but that would be the single that would finally break the band into the mainstream all over the world.

I said my goodbyes to everybody and told them I would see them in two weeks in San Francisco on the Lollapalooza tour… and in sunny weather!!

Left: Arik looks a bit nervous on his first gig
and slightly static on stage (below)
Top right: Arik, slightly more relaxed the next day
Top, far right: Anthony backstage caked in mud

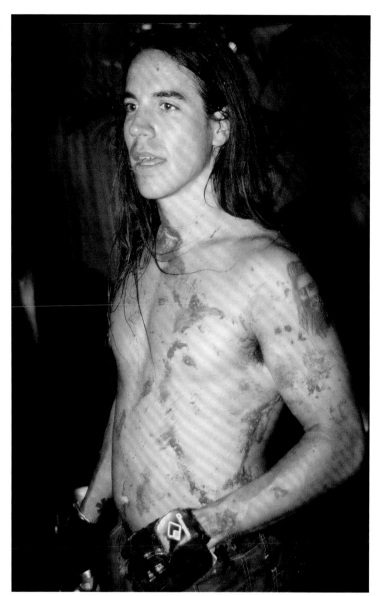

Right: Anthony with tattooist, Henky Penky Below: Getting in the groove to some funk music in the dressing room

LOLLAPALOOZA
PALO ALTO, SAN FRANCISCO
BOWLER HATS TO FLAMING HELMETS

The summer of 1992 saw Lollapalooza, America's biggest travelling festival, tour again with a completely different line-up to the year before. The festival brainchild of Perry Farrel (Jane's Addiction, Porno for Pyros) the tour caused big news in the US in '91 - selling out instantly. Never had America seen such a diverse line-up put together on one bill, with the likes of Ice T playing with the Butthole Surfers, The Rollins Band and Siouxsie and the Banshees, Living Colour and the headline act on their last ever tour – Jane's Addiction. It was a massive success and this year's line-up was even stronger with the Chili Peppers headlining. Also on the bill were Ministry, Soundgarden, Pearl Jam, Ice Cube and The Charlatans, to name a few. On one of the smaller side stages were Porno for Pyros and the Jim Rose Circus of Scars (a gruesome freak show which included stomach bile drinking and eating light bulbs).

AK hitches a ride from a member of the Boo-Yaa T.R.I.B.E

Come show time for the Chili Peppers their new stage set was unveiled to the crowd, the centre piece being a giant rotating circle. Anthony was dressed in a black and white checked suit complete with bowler hat and sunglasses for the first couple of songs, before stripping the suit off. Arik's first gig on US soil went down great. For the encore the band returned on stage with giant naked flames blazing out of their steel safety helmets which were running off a propane gas bottle strapped around their waists. The only drawback of this effect was that after a short while the helmets tended to get rather hot. It was a really great end to a good first day at the festival.

The next day, the Peppers again played a great set, but on their encore the Boo-Yaa T.R.I.B.E. – a Samoan rap band from LA, who were playing one of the smaller stages at the festival – joined them on stage. One of the band – a huge guy – picked Anthony up and sat him on his shoulder for the entire song.

I said my goodbyes to the band and as I left the US, 'Under the Bridge' was just beginning to get heavy rotation on MTV.

WOODSTOCK 1994
LIGHT BULBS GO ON FOR DAVE'S DEBUT

In 1993 Dave Navarro, ex-Jane's Addiction guitarist, joined the Peppers. I was excited to hear this news, as I was a massive fan of Jane's and was looking forward to hearing what Dave and the band would come up with musically. In the summer of '94 a massive event was planned for the 25th anniversary of the Woodstock festival. It was to be held very close to the original site in Upstate New York over the weekend of August 3rd and 4th with a smaller opening event on the Friday night. A lot of massive acts were playing, among them Metallica, Nine Inch Nails, Aerosmith, Green Day, Primus, Blind Melon and Bob Dylan. The Red Hot Chili Peppers were scheduled to close the entire event on the Sunday night. This would be Dave Navarro's first show with the band.

It had been raining hard most of the week and the site was a muddy bog when we arrived. There was no cover for the photographers at the front of the stage and our equipment was getting very wet while we shot the first three songs of each of our acts that we had to cover. My friend and fellow photographer Mark Leialoha from San Fran was hit by a large bag of mud. I gave up every dry duster and rag to help him try and clean his gear.

I didn't think it could get any worse until waiting for Saturday's headline act – Aerosmith – to come on stage, there was a delay as a huge thunder and lightning storm had centred over the festival. The PA was warning everybody to keep low to the ground to avoid lightning strikes. You can imagine how this went down with 400,000 people; yes, even I panicked a little. I eventually shot my three Aerosmith songs and got out of there with Mark.

The next day, returning in Mark's car, we were stopped by the police 10 miles from the site and they told us we would have to park up and walk the rest of the way because too many people were trying to leave and they were only allowing vehicles out and not in. We walked and walked and it seemed forever, especially carrying heavy camera equipment.

Finally getting to the site I managed to catch tour manager Tony. He informed me that he didn't have my all-areas pass for the Peppers but would sort it out. I had a long wait until finally, just before they were about to go on, I got the message to meet him by the stage entrance and as soon as he got the band on stage he would hand me my pass. They came on wearing massive light bulb suits for their first number and I only just managed to click off a few frames as soon as I got my pass as there wasn't much of the song left. I said hello to Chad, who stuck his tongue out to me happily drumming away (which made a change from flipping me the finger!) and shot the rest of their set from the side of the stage.

The band played a couple of new tracks I hadn't heard before which had just been written with Dave, Aeroplane being one of them. Dave seemed to fit in perfectly with the band and they went down great with the crowd. He always had a real stage presence when he was with Jane's.

Anthony, at one point, had everybody swinging their t-shirts above their heads for an entire number, which looked amazing with the 200,000-odd people still there – considering what a long weekend it had been.

My lift back to the hotel was with Mark, who had kindly gone on ahead after three Peppers songs - walking back the 10 miles to fetch the car and come and pick me up. I left early just before the band's encore to get to Mark and missed them playing in their Jimmy Hendrix suits as an encore tribute to him. A disaster from start to finish. 'If I never shoot that festival again – thank God' were my thoughts as we drove off into the night…

Left: Dave feeling a bit light headed on his debut... it's not easy playing with a two-foot bulb on your bonce, and he wasn't thrilled with the idea
Above: Shit happens. Mark after his mud bath

How many crew members does it take to change a light bulb?

ONE HOT MINUTE
UK TOUR 1996

NAVARRO'S SECRET. MADONNA BACKSTAGE. FLYING DRUMSTICKS

In September, 1995 the band finally released a new album, their first with Dave Navarro on guitar, and follow-up to BloodSugarSexMagik. Although a lot darker and heavier in parts than the band's previous albums it was released with great reviews from the UK music press (the ones that mattered!)

In October they headed to Europe for their first dates in over a year and the first part of the One Hot Minute tour, which would start in the UK. I suddenly found myself in a strange place, photography wise, with Raw, the magazine I freelanced regularly for over a period of five or so years, changing musical direction. I found myself looking for a new magazine to shoot for. Salvation came in Kerrang, the

UK's biggest rock magazine. They asked if I would be interested in working for them. I jumped at the chance. I immediately paid back Kerrang's faith in me by covering a Chili Peppers show that no-one else was allowed in to shoot. It was a secret show set up by the band as a fundraiser for a friend and fellow musician at home in the US by the name of D.H. Peligro, a drummer from LA who had a serious accident at home and was having a bad time. This show was at Subterainia, a small venue, just off Portobello Road in London, and was announced on the day of the gig, and sold out in seconds.

I went down to see everybody at the sound check. It had been quite a while since I had spoken to any of the band, but I was greeted with warm smiles and hand shakes by all of them, which made me feel like I was home straight away. There were now a couple of new crew guys on the tour. Dave's guitar tech was a great guy by the name of Dave Lee who I got on with straight away.

The gig was packed and extremely hard to shoot simply as there was no photo pit. I found myself having to muscle in with the crowd to get the best shots I could. It was extremely hot and sweaty, but a great little club gig. In fact this was the smallest gig I had seen the band play at this point. Anthony was donning a French maid's outfit, which became his stage clothes for the rest of the UK tour.

The next shows were at the normal bigger venues like two nights at Brixton Academy which were brilliant. I finally got to know Dave better at these shows and found him a great guy. He enjoyed reading and looking at the shots from Kerrang and the Subterainia show. He had a dark sense of humour that I found quite funny. The first thing I picked up on was the guitar plectrums that he had. On the back of his was the list of names of the entire previous Chili Peppers guitarists – there was a question mark after his own name!

On the first night at Brixton, Dave suddenly approached me waving his hand to stop taking pictures of him playing halfway through the set. I immediately thought I had pissed him off in some way and was in two minds what to do. At the end of the song Dave came up to the front of the pit and knelt down to say something to me. It turned out the guitar he was playing was a loan trial guitar and he did not want any shots taken of it as he thought it looked like Prince's guitar and didn't like it. Panic over, I carried on.

Flea's old flame decides to strip off and dance... getting me into trouble
Left: Dave bonds with the crowd after the first night at Brixton

On the second night an unexpected guest showed up, whisked in through a side entrance with her bodyguard. It was Madonna, who was in town recording the sound track to Evita. She was escorted backstage to have a chat with the band. I found it quite odd standing next to her in the corridor in the Academy while the band went on stage.

Later that night something happened to me that Chad Smith found hilarious. On the encore song Flea's then girlfriend decided to strip off and dance topless with the band on stage whilst they played Suffragette City, a track by David Bowie. I was pleasantly going about my task taking pictures in the pit at the front. Suddenly I felt a blow to the top of my head that came from nowhere. I immediately turned around to the fans at the front row behind the barrier and asked in no polite terms who had hit me with something. They all denied any knowledge of doing so, which made me even happier, as you can imagine. Suddenly something hit me in the back hard, as I had turned my back to the band. I turned around and looked and there, lying on the floor, was a drumstick. I looked up to see Chad laughing his head off, not missing a beat while firing drumsticks at me, crashing them off the cymbals. I mouthed something at Chad that I cannot repeat here in writing, which made him laugh even more.

I got some great shots of Flea's girlfriend on stage dancing with the band, one shot of which I did a print for her… which she gave to her father!

At the Manchester Apollo show I got a few of my friends in to see the band for the first time. I think they were surprised when Anthony mentioned my name on stage, saying "Be careful when you surf over the crowd how you land in the pit, don't worry if you land on Tony Woolliscroft though, he's just a photographer!" My friends all thought this was hilarious. Nice thought, I thanked him afterwards.

*Top: Navarro at your service.
It's hot and sweaty in Subterainia
and Dave cools the girls down
with a glass of water
Second right: Dave has a Prince
moment over his guitar
Far right: Various shots from the
One Hot Minute Tour including
Chad (bottom left corner) playing
Dave's guitar with his drumsticks
at the end of the
Manchester Apollo gig*

EAST COAST
HOODS ON HEADS AND SOCKS ON COCKS

The band's US tour started in Philadelphia in February '96. I arrived in New York on that first date so planned to go to Boston for the show the night after. It was freezing, snow everywhere. When I got to the venue it was early afternoon and Tony the TM immediately put me to work in the production office sorting out the guest list and passes for that night's show, until the band arrived.

The guys were now really getting into a great groove live, Dave looking like he had been with them for years. They were even throwing little snippets of Jane's Addiction songs into their set, which made me smile to myself. Boston was another great show, with backing singers Rain Phoenix (River's sister) and old crew member and good friend Robbie, still on the tour.

I travelled back to New York on the crew bus. Still a bit jet lagged. I was asleep before we left the venue for the long drive to Manhattan for the show the following day.

I awoke the following morning and got off the bus to be faced with the sight of the Empire State Building looking fantastic on a cold winter's day. This show was quite a big deal as it was the Peppers' first time headlining the famous and sold-out New York Madison Square Gardens. I was again put to work in the production office sorting guest passes out for the show which everybody and their long lost cousins wanted to be at.

I shot a few pictures of Dave soundchecking in the empty venue in the afternoon. Myself and Chad went out into the crowd just to have a look around the massive venue early on, Chad having to retreat after only a few minutes as he was being mobbed for autographs. The show itself was a triumph. One of the highlights was Iggy Pop's guest appearance for the encore singing 'I Wanna Be Your Dog' – an old Iggy Pop and the Stooges number. AK climbed high up the lighting rig ladder then took a huge jump into mid air... Flea playing till his long white pants nearly fell off.

I met up with the band two days later at the 'Ed Sullivan Theatre' on Broadway as they were appearing live on the David Letterman show early that evening to promote their new single: 'Aeroplane'. In soundcheck the band made everybody laugh, including David Letterman, about the parker coats they were wearing while playing. Now you must remember that it was winter in the US at this time and cold on the East coast with it, so you would expect to be going into a warm TV studio to play a live broadcast, but not the David Letterman show. Apparently he keeps the studio very cold all year round, as he does not like to sweat while interviewing his guests under the warm studio lights, so the band played their song live on TV wearing their Parker coats zipped up with the hoods on! Backstage we met actor Jackie Chan who was also a guest on the show and seemed like a nice guy.

*Looking cool and staying warm:
Dave and backing singer Robbie
in the Letterman studios (left)*

I did two more shows with the band the following week in upstate NY – Albany and Rochester (amazed to find that place a dry town on a Sunday where no alcohol could be bought or consumed!)

On the last date on the East Coast leg at Nassau Coliseum, Long Island, I'd organised a photo shoot with the band before they went on stage and set it up backstage in one of the dressing rooms. I learnt a lesson that day. AK took me to one side after what was a short shoot and explained that the band, after all this time, did not like long photo shoots. He said if I wanted to cover them properly I should concentrate on documenting my time with them, including backstage and everything else that was going on, in which case I would come away with a lot more pictures and not just have to rely on the band doing photo sessions all the time.

Tour support for this leg had come from an Australian act called Silverchair, who at this point were a really young three-piece who had their dads as crew guys on the road with them. The Peppers had organised some strippers to

come out for Silverchair's last song, and the lads' fathers thought this was hilarious. When the two girls did walk on stage the young band didn't quite no what to do, and two of them actually ran off stage. Everybody found it funny - even Silverchair in the end.

I shot another great show and was now used to climbing up on Chad's drum riser with him as they played the final song in their set to get a fisheye shot of Chad, the whole band, and the large venues with the full crowd in the picture.

It was encore time and something quite unexpected happened. Tony the TM came running out of the band's dressing room just before they were due to return to the stage. "They're doing Socks on Cocks," said Tony as he ran past me to get one more new pair of white tube socks for a band member. I had never witnessed them do this in all the gigs I had seen and it was somewhat of a rarity now. Luckily I had two rolls of film left from my entire trip, just enough to cover the song while the band played. The strippers joined the band on stage at the end, AK's sock

Pop idol: Iggy joins the guys on stage for the encore at Madison Square Gardens Right-hand page: Soundcheck on the day and the guys were all pretty excited about playing that night

coming dangerously close to falling off at one point and adjustment was needed. Even Robbie (backing singer) was butt naked except for the sock, fair to say that Rain kept her clothes on. Silverchair getting in on the act to help Chad smash his drum kit up right as the last note played. It was a great way to finish the East Coast leg of the tour.

After the show I got a lift back into Manhattan with the band on their bus. Flea and Dave played cards all the way back, the rest of the band just relaxing as we journeyed through the snow-lined streets. At the band's hotel in Midtown I said my goodbyes and told them I would see them again in the summer in Europe for the festivals.

045

I said put a sock in it... not ON it!

050

EUROPEAN FESTIVALS
MORE RUMOURS. FLEA GETS BUTT NAKED

In July of '96 the band returned to Europe to play the festival circuit and one final date in the UK on this album tour at Wembley Arena. I decided to go out to the last weekend of the band's festival dates, which were in Torhout and Werchter, Belgium, praying we wouldn't see any more mud. Strange thing was that rumours were circulating yet again that all was not right in the band and the mood in the dressing room was not great. It was a marked difference this time around. The weather was fantastic, wall-to-wall sunshine. On the bill were Rage Against The Machine, Alanis Morissette and Neil Young, to mention just a few.

I arrived backstage to find the atmosphere very relaxed, no tension at all. Anthony was in quite a lot of discomfort though. A fall at a previous festival show on to a stage monitor had hurt the lower part of his back quite badly and he was having to wear a large white back support. This obviously restricted his movement – not great for a guy who was used to moving and leaping around the stage.

In the band's dressing room Flea and Dave jammed together. They played a rousing rendition of the Sex Pistols' 'God Save The Queen'. Even Tony the tour manager was getting in on the jam playing an extra bass guitar. If there was tension in the camp it was being very well hidden at this point.

Myself, Flea and Dave went up to the side of the stage to watch Rage Against The Machine, who were very impressive, whipping the crowed up into a frenzy during their set.

Flea doesn't have to
worry about Pepper spray...
Top left: Catching 40 winks
Middle, left: Tony, the TM, plays God
Save The Queen with Dave Navarro
Bottom left: Knock, knock...
it's a camera crew

Come stage time for the band Flea played the first couple of numbers wearing an old gas mask, then he decided to strip totally stark naked and played the rest of the set. The band went down a storm. Nobody could quite believe what Flea had done.

The next show in Werchter was much the same, sunshine and very relaxed backstage. I took a picture of Chad and two other drumming buddies together, Igor from Sepultura and a young Taylor Hawkins who was then playing with Alanis Morissette, soon to become the drummer for the Foo Fighters. Again, Flea played the set butt naked, but from the beginning this time, the band going down a storm.

The gig at Wembley was the biggest show the band had played in the UK as a solo act. It sold out immediately. John Curd the promoter said they probably could have played another night and sold that out as well. The band was becoming very big news in the UK, the album selling well, and it was good to see.

Still at this time rumours persisted that all was not right in the band so when Kerrang sent a journalist to interview them that was the angle he went for. Interviewing each of the guys individually he asked the same question each time: 'were the band going home to split up?' Just to play along with this, they all gave the same answer… "yes!".

Paul, the journalist, had realised that the band were taking the piss in the interview so he was none the wiser in the end. Actually it made quite a funny read in the issue. I managed to get the band to do a quick shoot with me for the feature this time. I got it done in six minutes!

The show was excellent, even though AK was still in a lot of discomfort with his back injury. On the final song of the set both Chad and Dave completely trashed their equipment. Navarro leaving his guitar sticking vertically out of his speaker amp lying flat on the stage floor. This gig was the first time that I took my then girlfriend Ange and our best friend Lees to see the band. They were well looked after by Tony the TM and were given VIP passes for the show. Actually Dave Navarro made Lees' night by giving her a cheeky wink and wave as he walked passed her back stage, she didn't shut up about it all the way home.

Dave's last stand...

MT FUJI ROCK FESTIVAL, JAPAN 1997
GIVING ANTHONY A BELT. NAVARRO TAKES ON A TYPHOON

The band played one date only in '97, headlining the inaugural Mt Fuji Rock Festival in Japan. I approached the record company to try and get some money towards the cost of the trip, flights to Tokyo and hotels wouldn't be cheap – but as the band had no new album out and nothing to promote I got no for an answer. Just after I went ahead and bought my air ticket I got some really bad news. While riding his motorbike in LA, Anthony had been knocked off and had seriously damaged his wrist. His arm was now in a cast past the elbow and it was touch and go whether or not he would be allowed to do the show. I had a very nervous wait for a couple of weeks. Finally he got the green light from his doctors with certain conditions (more on that later) and I was a relieved man.

I flew to Tokyo on the Thursday and arrived on the Friday afternoon, staying in Shinjuku, which made Times Square, NY, look dull. An early start was needed the following day to catch the bus to the festival which was located halfway up Mt Fuji – quite a distance from Tokyo. While the weather had been dull in Tokyo there was no sign of rain, but the nearer we got to Fuji the weather was changing, and by the time the bus dropped us all off at the festival it was coming down hard. The word was that a typhoon was coming in fast and would hit the festival site around Saturday night – everybody was keeping a close eye on the weather reports through the day, hoping that the storm would miss us.

On the bill on the Saturday were the Foo Fighters, Rage Against the Machine and a number of Japanese bands I had never heard of. The Peppers were due to close the show. While shooting the Foo Fighters the weather was getting progressively worse. Rain and high winds were beginning to lash the festival. I shot the Foos from the side of the stage.

The Peppers arrived and I went to their dressing room to drop my equipment off and say hello. Despite persistent

rumours that things were not good in the camp again everybody seemed very relaxed and in good spirits. I spoke to AK about his motorbike accident; he said his doctors had given him the all clear to play the show as long as he kept the plaster cast dry – by the time the band hit the stage there was little chance of that!

Throughout the afternoon different bands popped in to the Peppers' dressing room to say hello. I got some good shots with Keith Flint from the Prodigy (They were due to play the next day, but came to the festival a day early as Maxim and Keith got up and performed with Rage Against the Machine for one number). I worked steadily documenting the band's day backstage. In between all this I had to do a photo session with The Foo Fighters which coincided with Rage Against the Machine performing. That proved quite tricky and I found myself running to the stage just to catch a couple of numbers of Rage's set. Luckily one of the numbers I shot was the one with Keith and Maxim singing with them and I got some good images.

The rain was torrential now and, as night time fell upon the gig, fears were beginning to grow that it might get called off. A decision was made to move all the equipment further back on the stage away from the front which was getting more and more soaked from the storm. At least this would allow the bands to play.

In the Peppers' dressing room things were relaxed, both Flea and Dave warming-up playing their guitars, then we heard the news that the festival organisers were making a decision whether or not to abandon for the day. The Peppers made it clear that they wanted to play, or at least try to. The organisers agreed and the band's equipment was set up, again well back from the front of the stage to at least give them a chance to play. AK was worried about the cast on his arm getting too wet and maybe it would need some support. Nobody had a spare belt to offer him so I took mine off my shorts and he used that.

I made a decision to try and shoot at least three songs from the photo pit at the front of the stage. As the band finally came on the weather got worse. All fears were confirmed and we were now in the middle of a full-on typhoon, named Rosa. It was horrendous. I lasted just one song at the front – my equipment was getting too soaked. It was hopeless – rain running into my eyes. I couldn't see. I went on stage to try and get cover and some better shots, pulling my shorts up on the way worried it would be me doing my own version of 'Sock on Cock' as the rain lashed down…

On stage things weren't much better. High winds were driving the rain on to the band. I tried to take some pictures of Chad who was furthest away at the back. At this point there was that much water running down my lens it was having trouble focusing on him playing the drums. That's how bad it was. There was one picture among all of this I regret not taking - the wind was so bad four crew members were having to hold Flea and Dave's backline speakers up on each side of the stage to prevent them from being blown over.

After 25 minutes a decision was made to pull the band off for fears that one of them would be electrocuted. Stage lights from the lighting rig above the band were now hanging just by their wires after being battered by the storm for so long.

Finally, the band reluctantly came off stage. Dave was the last, he really did not want to go. As he stood there on his own trying to take on a typhoon, maybe he knew something we didn't. It turned out be his last gig with the band. In April '98 he left.

Top left: Dave wanted his name in Japanese on his chest for the gig
Top: Flea checks out his bass muscles
Above: Trashing the equipment at the end of the set
Left: Anthony strapped up for the ride

Top: Anthony trades tales with the Prodigy's Keith Flint
Above: A fan is stretchered away as the storm wreaks havoc
Right: Mirror, mirror on the wall... Chad's the fairest of them all
Top right: Tom Merello of Rage Against The Machine drops in for a chat
Bottom right: Flea checks out his per diems (festival pocket money)

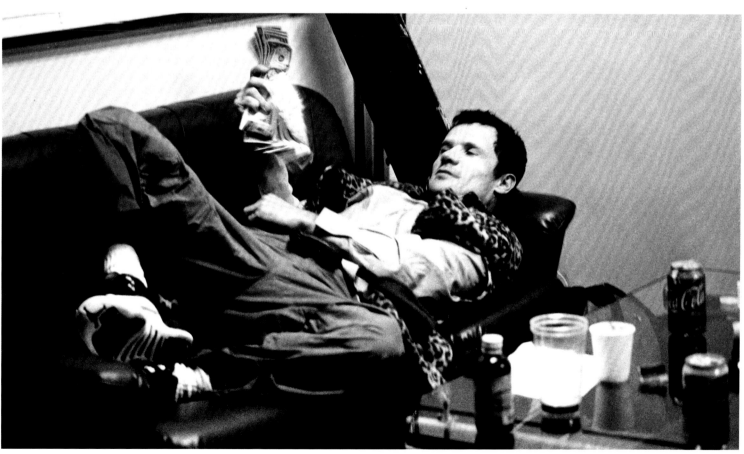

Throw it away now: Anthony launches the guitar in the direction of guitar tech, Dave Lee, after playing a few bars on Give It Away at Washington RFK Stadium

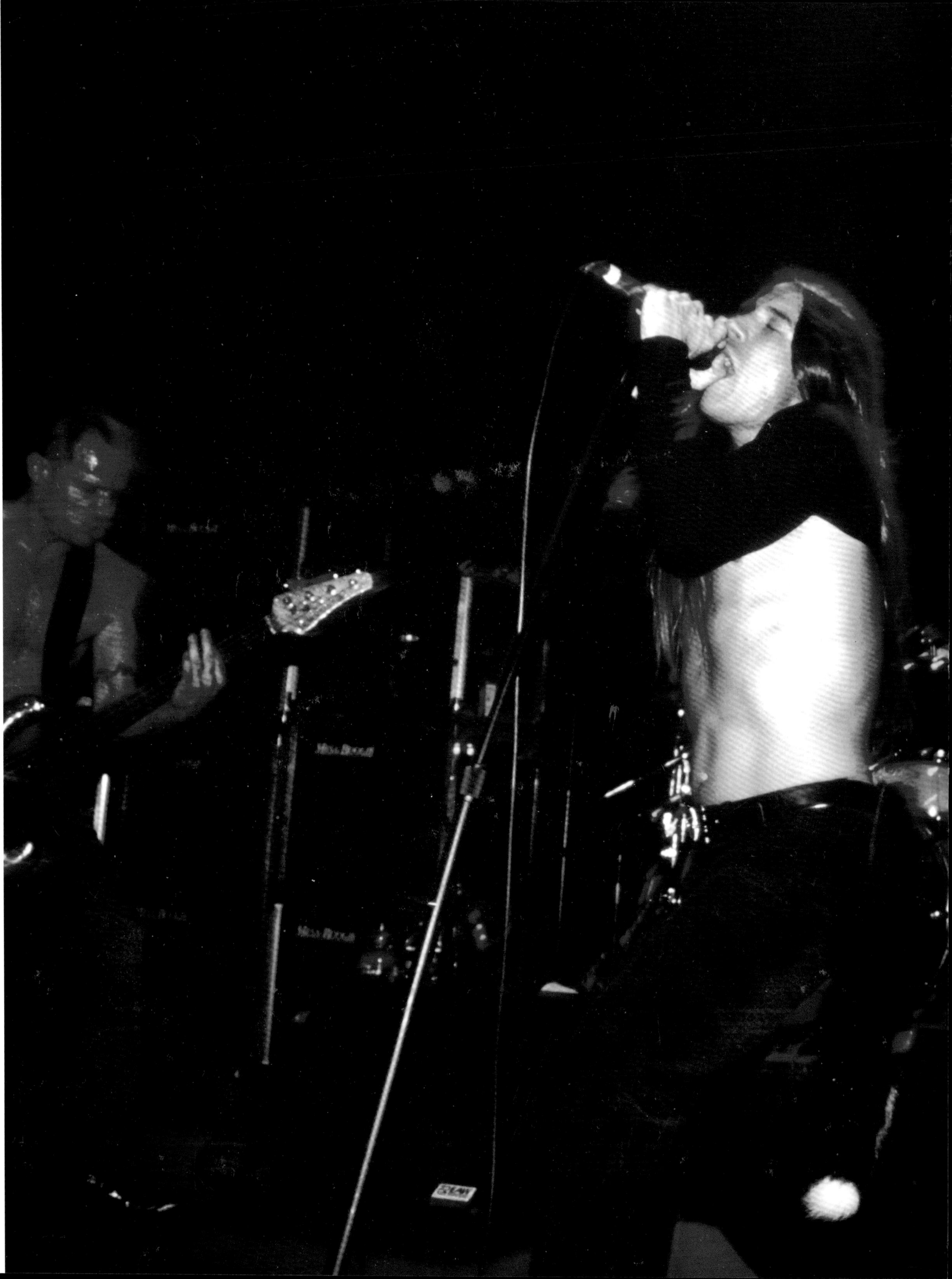

WASHINGTON 9.30 CLUB & TIBETAN FREEDOM CONCERT, WASHINGTON RFK STADIUM
JOHN'S RETURN.
WEATHERING THE STORM WITH CHAD.
PEARL GET THE GUYS OUT OF A JAM

In April of '98 John Frusciante rejoined the Chili Peppers, and in July of that year they announced their first gigs. They had been a last minute addition to this year's Tibetan Freedom concert at the RFK Stadium in Washington DC. They also announced a small warm-up show at the 9.30 club in DC. At this point the band had not had any new music out for nearly three years, so yet again there was absolutely no chance of getting any money out of the record company to help me pay for the trip.

On the day of the secret 9.30 Club show I met the band in their hotel reception at 2.00pm for the short journey to the soundcheck. I walked straight past John – I really didn't recognise him. I hadn't seen him for five years, and to be truthful didn't know him as well as the other guys. He had changed quite a bit. I said my hellos to the band and Tony Sellinger the TM re-introduced me to John. In the van on the short journey to the club Tony told us that tonight's gig had sold out in record time with the phone lines nearly going into meltdown when it was announced who the band was playing a warm-up gig. I chatted to AK about his wrist, as I hadn't seen him since Japan. He explained he had lost some mobility in the wrist but other than that he was ok. I shot the soundcheck at the club then interviewed AK back at the hotel for Kerrang, which was really interesting as I'd never actually sat down and interviewed him before.

The show that night was very funky, but mellow. It was a great set and there were songs that I hadn't heard them play before like 'Soul to Squeeze'. It set the scene nicely for the gig the following day at RFK Stadium and the Tibetan Freedom concert.

SATURDAY. RFK STADIUM

I woke up to blue skies over Washington and got in the van to go to the gig. I documented as much stuff as I could backstage following Flea around as he did his MTV duties interviewing the crowd. The day was going fine, then around mid-afternoon everything changed. It went very dark then the sky went black! Next thing there was a massive crack as a bolt of lightning hit the stadium. A torrential downpour followed. Backstage was a washout, the tents erected as dressing rooms nearly blowing over, everybody running for cover and taking shelter under the stadium itself. I stood and waited for the storm to pass with Chad. Half an hour later we were still waiting there. My lasting memory from that time was looking at Chad's face when I asked him what it was with thunder storms and bad weather at outdoor festivals with this band as we took shelter? I can't possibly tell you his reply in print.

A decision was eventually made to cancel the rest of the day's concert as news filtered through that somebody had been badly injured when the stadium was struck by lightning and was in hospital. We were told all bands that hadn't played today would be added to the bill tomorrow. Chad and myself got a lift back to the hotel with Pearl Jam.

Soundcheck:
John takes a moment
to drink it all in...
that familiar feeling
of being back with the band,
while AK enjoys a quick
smoke (left)

SUNDAY

On arriving at the stadium the band were told they wouldn't be able to play as they had been a last minute add-on to the original line-up and there was no room for them. After many fruitless protests by the band and personnel, everybody was gutted, but not in the mood to be defeated. A little later in the afternoon a plan was hatched. Pearl Jam, who had toured regularly with the Peppers early on in their careers, agreed to give up 20 minutes of their set so the Peppers could at least get to play. The bare basics of the guys' equipment was moved to the side of the stage so that when Pearl Jam walked off guitars and pedals were plugged in and they sneaked on stage! The crowd went mad and the band went for it. It was an amazing, short, intense set. They went down brilliantly. It was a great welcome back to John! Next morning we said our goodbyes in the hotel reception. The band were travelling on to New York and a gig there. I was homeward bound.

Top left: That's Flea in the corner... with Michael Stipe
Above and centre: Flea interviews fans for MTV
and catches up with Eddie Vedder of Pearl Jam

CALIFORNICATION 1999

COVERED WITH PRIDE

In 1999 the band released Californication – their first album with John Frusciante back on guitar – to rave reviews. I was especially proud. On the inside sleeve was my shot of the band in a huddle taken in Washington the year before. I was really pleased that it was the guys themselves who wanted to use the shot.

In the summer of '99 the band headed to Europe for some secret shows and press work. I made my way over to Paris to shoot their show at the Elysee Monmartre, a small club not far from the famous Moulin Rouge.

I bumped into AK at the band's hotel. I was amazed at how different he looked. Gone was his long hair – now replaced with a short blond crop. We chatted in the car ride to the club about the VH1 'Behind The Music' programme on the band, which I had supplied pictures for.

We arrived at the gig. There was bedlam outside – hundreds of people after non-existent tickets. The first person to greet me was Chad who gave me a big hug. It was great to see him. I set about taking documentary shots backstage which included JF playing Flea's bass and Flea playing JF's guitar. The show was hot beyond belief in the small club, the band playing a great set for the enthusiastic Parisian crowd.

Left: Sorting the set list for the secret show in Paris

RADIO ONE, UK

A few days later I was at the Radio One studios in London for the band's live broadcast on the Simon Mayo show. They had a brief rehearsal in the studio before going live, performing Soul To Squeeze and their single Scar Tissue. They also recorded 'Emit Remus' which was broadcast at a later date. I documented the whole thing – one of the shots was used on the sleeve of the 'Around the World' single cd cover. The broadcast went without a hitch, with Flea deciding to make the bizarre announcement: "Tonight at midnight there will be a special meeting at Catford Cemetery, where they will be running around the church counter clockwise."

TFI FRIDAY

Straight after the Radio One session we moved down to Hammersmith and to Chris Evans' TFI Friday programme, a chat show and music programme, live every Friday night at 6pm. Also on were Aerosmith who were sound-checking, Steve Tyler later walking around the triangular shaped stage to watch the Peppers do their sound check. I got some shots and walked with the band to their dressing room, which was strangely situated in a terraced house across the road, the band having to run the gauntlet of fans waiting for autographs.

At performance time, I went with the band into the studio and waited for them to be introduced. As soon as they started playing I managed one picture before being stopped by security because no one had informed them that I was with the band… Great!

082

NEW SINGLE
LIGHTNING SE
25TH GLASGOW
27TH WOLVERH
30TH YORK BA
2ND BRISTOL C
5TH NORWICH
13TH & 14TH LIV

Relaxing backstage at TFI Friday. It was a terraced house across the road from the set and was a bit of a dump but the guys didn't seem too bothered

CAMDEN PALACE

We quickly moved on from the TV studio to Camden Palace for the band's next secret show. I had been asked by Rhythm magazine to shoot pictures of Chad for a drumming feature. While we got some nice portrait pictures backstage we had to go out into the club to take some shots of Chad on his drum kit while it was filling up. He took it all in his stride, posing around his kit as I snapped away. I also took some ring flash pictures of AK backstage. The atmosphere was very relaxed back there as the band waited for show time, which, once again, was fantastic.

Chad stickin' it to the camera...
and no flippin' the finger for a change

YONGE STREET, TORONTO
EXPENSES AT LAST... BUT
CHAD FORGETS HIS WALLET

The band were due to give a free concert in Toronto at the HMV record store in Yonge Street on the 22nd of July, three days before their Woodstock 30th anniversary headlining date on Sunday the 25th. It was my first trip anywhere to shoot the Peppers not paid for by myself! I was looking forward to it as I felt like there was a big push being made around the band at this time, and album sales were beginning to prove it. I was genuinely excited to go out and shoot the guys. It was a great time to be around them as the mood was so positive.

I hooked up with them at their hotel just in time to watch Chad accidentally knock AK's nice pair of sunglasses off his head and off the hotel roof – where the band were doing a photo shoot with a Canadian magazine – never to be seen again. The band had paired up to do the various TV interviews. I stayed with AK and Chad, who in their first stint went into a fantastic introduction to the band for the camera. It was a brilliant monologue which had everybody in stitches… then the cameraman realised he had not loaded a tape. Oh dear! It happens to the best of us. Trust me, he took some stick for that. Shame really because the off-the-cuff introduction they did they couldn't do again.

On the way to watch a movie with Chad, (Run Lola Run), we rode down to reception in the elevator with Jimmy Smits, an actor who was in town filming a movie. He didn't really have a lot to say. When we got to the theatre Chad realised he had forgotten his wallet... yeah that old chestnut – and I had to pay for both of us to watch the film. There I was on a trip where the record company had finally paid, but Chad was still taxing me in other ways! I gave him some stick over it. Meeting up with AK before the gig in reception of the hotel, we talked movies and quickly realised we had gone to see the wrong film and should have opted to see 'American Beauty' instead... Chad joked he didn't pay anyway!

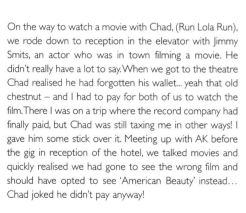

I travelled with the crew to Yonge Street and to the outdoor stage that had been erected opposite the HMV store on the street. It was filling with people, and this was with two hours to go until the band were due to play. With one hour to go the police actually shut the area down and were not allowing anybody else within a half-mile radius. I saw fans on a multi-storey car park two streets away trying to see the gig through a gap in the buildings. It was chaos, with people climbing lampposts, street signs and just about anything that they could get a good view from.

Backstage and dressing room for the band was a tour bus parked behind the stage. Flea was wearing a kaftan. It turns out this was the only thing he had to play in at the time, as the airline had mislaid his luggage.

Come show time I started taking pictures from the small pit at the front of the stage. I had to time everything right really. With it being a free gig the band were only playing six or seven songs at the most, so my plan was to shoot two songs out front in the pit, two songs on stage, then get to the HMV rooftop ASAP to shoot two songs with a stunning view of the stage and street. Of course nothing went to plan. I got some great shots out front including a great one of Flea in mid air, and AK with his new stage clothes – a white shirt, black tie and black shorts. I then got up on stage and stood on Chad's drum riser for a song shooting a real panoramic shot with my fisheye lens of the band, stage, crowd and street. Things were going well until I tried to make my way across the street to the store and rooftop. It was so packed I got stuck halfway and couldn't get any further and, worse still, I couldn't get back either. It physically took me one and a half songs to get nowhere.

Afterwards the band did some TV around the stage area. Mingling with the crowd, they signed autographs and did interviews. One crazy person brought his pet iguana with him and wanted the band to sign it, which they all refused.

Finished for the evening the guys retreated to their hotel and later went out for a meal. I was shattered as I'd been up since 3.30am and went back to my hotel to get some sleep ready for the short flight down to Syracuse, NY State in the morning and the Woodstock festival.

At around lunchtime the mini bus called at our hotel for the crew and myself for the short ride to the airport. The band were already there, checked in, and we all gathered at the departure gate. It was at this point that Flea grabbed the tannoy mic and announced something about me over the public address system. I was still half asleep. All I can remember is hearing my name over the loud speaker and everybody in fits of laughter! It was only a very short run to Syracuse airport and John spent the flight strumming his acoustic guitar while AK stood and chatted to Flea most of the way.

WOODSTOCK FESTIVAL 1999
NO SMOKE WITHOUT FIRE

The band was yet again the headline act on the final day of the three-day festival. They arrived mid-afternoon and were immediately whisked away to do various interviews for magazines and MTV. Afterwards they retired to their dressing room. Anthony began working out the band's set list for the evening show, while Flea had a quick nap.

Later on, early evening time, Flea had a visitor. Jimmy Hendrix's sister popped into the dressing room to ask a special favour. She wondered if the band would finish their set that evening with the Hendrix song 'Fire' as a

hologram of Jimmy Hendrix was due to be shown on stage to finish the whole weekend. At this point the band had not played the song with John for over eight years. A meeting was called and after three quick rehearsals in the practice room the song was added as the last in the set that night. The band then went through their pre-gig rituals of yoga stretches and vocal exercises. I managed one very quick roll of film for a session before they went on stage.

Flea decided to play completely naked for the whole show, incredibly risky in terms of arrest considering it was being televised live on a pay-per-view channel. The band walked on stage under a glorious red sunset. Towards the end of their set, you could see from the stage that there was some sort of disturbance at the back of the crowd. As they played their last song a number of fires had been started with catering and vending carts ablaze. Apparently an angry mob were demonstrating to festival organisers over extortionate food and drink prices.

As soon as the band finished their set they were whisked away to beat the traffic and get to New York. The crew and myself witnessed a full-scale riot in progress, stuck at the festival, unable to leave until well into the early hours of the morning when order was restored.

Of course the next day the papers were full of the headlines that the Peppers played Fire as the crowd rioted. Of course they couldn't have been further from the truth, most of the press unaware why the band played the song.

Top right: Flea chats to Jimmy Hendrix's sister about playing 'Fire' as a tribute to her brother
Right: Untimely fires at Woodstock
Below: On the couch for an MTV interview

A sunset performance at Reading, and a quick picture before going on stage (below)

Flea's unorthodox approach to an encore at Leeds

READING AND LEEDS FESTIVAL 1999
STICK OFF CHAD OVER RUNAWAY AMPS

My lasting memory of the Reading Festival is nearly causing a disaster for the band. It was a great sunny afternoon and I had been documenting them from their arrival on the site. I'd even managed to get Mel C (Spice Girls) who had arrived with the band, to do a picture with a friend of mine, Pete from Sick Of It All (a New York Hardcore band) which ended up in Rolling Stone. She was a really nice person, signing autographs for anybody who asked, and had plenty of time for everybody.

Soon it was show time and I was busy taking pictures while the band played. As I kneeled down to get a good angle by the side of Chad I accidentally gave JF's backline (amps and speakers) a bit of a nudge. Next thing I know it's rolling across the stage towards John as he is playing… (I still say it was Dave's fault, as he didn't lock the wheels down on it!). Chris the production manager saved the day running across stage to stop the runaway stack! John didn't actually see the incident as he had his back to it all, facing the crowd, but NOT Chad. He gave me so much stick! He had the whole crew in stitches. He gave me so much abuse. I was dying. I was so embarrassed. As usual Chad never missed a beat as he was dishing it out. I think JF started laughing at all the crew laughing so much as Chad berated me. I'd never felt so bad. Afterwards, walking backstage into the dressing room, everybody again burst out laughing at me, which just made me feel worse. In the end I came round and stayed for a few hours and chatted while the traffic from the festival died down.

The next day in Leeds the weather was totally different. It was cold and wet and even though it was the same line-up the festival didn't seem to have the same spark as Reading the night before. The only thing that got the cold crowd going was Flea announcing that he had distant family relations in Bradford, then deciding to handstand across the stage naked for the band's encore entrance.

The other pictures shown are from Wembley and Den Haag, Holland, a few weeks later.

*Right: It looks like Flea's daughter
has told dad to put his dressing
gown on after his naked onstage
antics*

*Bottom right: No stars in the sky but
there's a full moon thanks to Chad*

*In a parallel universe:
Anthony gets away
from it all to sort out
the set list for Leeds*

102

*Final adjustments before
going on stage at Reading*

I took this picture of Anthony on the left when I did a fairly relaxed question and answer session with him for Kerrang. Here are some of the highlights:

What did 1999 mean to you?
AK:1999 was actually not profound for me because it was 1999. It just happened to be the year that we recorded this record, so the experience of being in a creative environment with John again after a long long time away from that made me realise that that was where I wanted to be, and that's who I wanted to make music with. And my girlfriend blossomed like a fucking flower from heaven, and I moved house.

Album of the year?
I don't know if it came out this year, but I can tell you what I discovered in 1999 and it became my favourite record, which was by Blonde Redhead. They're a band out of Washington DC. Two Italian guys who are kind of like in the Fugazi circle and it's a beautiful record.

Film of the year?
I would definitely say 'American Beauty'.

Wanker of the year?
That's a tough one, probably Liam Gallagher, just from the pictures I see of him in London, with the whole saint Liam thing.

What were you drinking this year?
My girlfriend.

Who was the sexiest person you met this year?
My girlfriend by far.

Who was the biggest tosser you met this year?
Well there was this guy today who was trying to sell me drugs in the street in Amsterdam. I made a joke about it, he was like asking me all these questions and I said: "unless you've got like a wheelbarrow full, don't even ask me 'cause you haven't got enough." I was joking and he looked at me like he wanted to kill me.

Where did you go on holiday this year?
I went on holiday this year to an island in the Caribbean, again with my girlfriend.

Personal high point of 1999?
Looking out the window of my aeroplane the other day looking at the clouds.

Personal low point of 1999?
I would say something, but it would just seem so trivial compared to like, the real low points that people experience.

Best band you've seen all year?
Well I did see some Fugazi shows this year that were off the hook. PJ Harvey I saw play in a record store that was very amazing.

Best song you wrote this year?
Well I was still writing songs when we were in the studio for our record and we actually finished the song Californication this year.

Weirdest fan experience of the year?
Well I had one tonight. I had this mailed package that was sent to the venue for me with tons of stamps on it and I think it was from England. It was a big tin box full of weed, which I don't smoke, with a little letter from a fan.

Most famous person you met this year?
I met Sean Penn.

Most extravagant thing you bought this year?
I wanted it be a house but I wasn't so lucky, so probably something for my girlfriend like a Gucci leather jacket.

Most trouble you got yourself into this year?
Again the fingers seem to be pointing towards my girlfriend 'cause it's very easy to get in trouble when you're on the road and communication becomes difficult when you don't call for a day. The other day she called up she asked for me and they put her through to a room of a woman and she thought she was getting my room and a woman picked up the phone.

Most outrageous thing you did this year?
The most outrageous thing would be joining up with the fellows in my band and wearing the Fela Kuti suits.

Favourite insult of 1999?
I will come back to that question.

Favourite chat-up line of 1999?
What's your sign?

The moment I most felt like a prize doughnut in 1999 was...
Well I did spend some time eating crispy creams in Washington Park in New York City.

'The Phantom Menace' – ace or arse?
Arse.

What will you be drinking on Xmas day 1999?
On Xmas day I will certainly be drinking tofu egg nog.

What will you be drinking on New Year's Eve?
I will probably be drinking a lot of air because we have a show that night in LA.

The year 2000 will include (hopes, dreams, aspirations, etc for the year ahead)...
A honeymoon in Venice, Italy, and lots of swimming in the ocean.

Chad shows off Henky Penky's latest work

WEMBLEY ARENA 1999
FELA KUTI SUITS AND BET I WAS HAPPY TO LOSE

The Peppers played their last UK date on the Californication tour in late November at Wembley arena.

They had some nice new stage outfits in the form of Fela Kuti suits. These brightly coloured two-piece outfits drew their inspiration from the famous African musician and human rights politician from Nigeria.

Chad had told me about them as we spoke in the afternoon. "Would be great to get a session shot of you guys before you go on stage," I suggested, knowing full well I had no hope of getting the band to pose for one. "I'll get them to do it," was Chad's reply. "Yeah right," was mine... "Put money on it," he countered, and so the bet was made.

Lo and behold, just as the band were about to go on in front of a sold-out Wembley, I heard my name being shouted by Chad from down the corridor where the band's dressing room was. I'd lost my bet. There they were. Chad had indeed got the band to pose for me for a few quick frames.

I laughed my head off as Chad gave me stick for not believing in him as we walked to the stage. The shots came in very handy as I had just interviewed AK and John for a Japanese magazine and thanks to Chad, I'd got the cover picture!

Melbourne set list, penned by Anthony, pictured doing pre-show press-ups (right)

BIG DAY OUT, AUSTRALIA
KUNG 'FOO' KICKS FROM CHAD

In January of 2000 I flew to Melbourne, Australia, for a week to shoot the Chili Peppers headlining the Big Day Out festival. This was Australia's premier music festival, which toured the country's major cities in the summer. It was nicknamed the Big Day Off by most bands on the bill as it could be up to five or six days between shows. On the bill this year with the Peppers were the Foo Fighters, Nine Inch Nails, Blink 182, the Helicopters and Joe Strummer and The Mescaleros. In addition to the festival date the Peppers were playing two nights at the massive Melbourne entertainment centre. Holding around 18,000 per night, they were both sold out.

On landing in Melbourne on the Friday morning, I was informed that the band were doing very little press at this point… this had me a little worried, as I had banked on getting a cover shot with Anthony and Foo Fighters frontman Dave Grohl together for a number of publications I was shooting for. I bumped into Dave Grohl first and asked if he was willing to do the shot with Anthony. No problem whatsoever, as long as we could do the shoot BEFORE the Peppers went on stage last thing at night as headliners. Ok, Anthony next… he says he'll do the shot as long as it's AFTER the Peppers set! Oh boy, I had one big problem.

DG had to fly back up to the Gold Coast for a court appearance to sort out a misdemeanour that had occurred on an earlier festival date. He had to be up by 5am to catch his flight and the Peppers would not be off stage until around midnight. After much pleading and begging with Gus Brandit, the Foo Fighters Tour Manager, he helped me out a great deal. DG (bless him) said he would hang around. After finally getting a quick shot of the two of them I retired back to my Punt Hill apartment shattered but happy that I had got everything.

The following week I shot the two Peppers shows, which I enjoyed far more than the Big Day Out gig, simply because it was just the Peppers on and nobody else. But I had a real treat on my penultimate night as the Foo Fighters were playing a secret show at the Hi-Fi club. As soon as the last goodnight was shouted at the Peppers gig I hightailed it across town and made it just as the Foo Fighters came on stage. Halfway through the Foo's set I felt a kick up my backside. Chad was standing there. "I thought I'd find you here" he laughed, then promptly jumped on stage and drummed along with Taylor for a number.

I flew home with my phone ringing non-stop. It turns out my picture of DG and AK together was in demand as both bands were playing together on the first leg of the Peppers' Californication tour in the US.

Flea just needs the
slippers to go with his
dressing gown after the
first night in Melbourne

Anthony with Dave Grohl from the Foo Fighters... cheers Dave, now go catch that plane

CALIFORNICATION USA TOUR
DRUMMING UP SUPPORT

The first major US tour for the Peppers came in spring after the Australian Big Day Out tour. The Foo Fighters were special guests. Chad loved this first leg of the tour, being big friends with the Foo camp, and every night he would join them on stage for one of their numbers. It was great to see all three drummers – Chad, Taylor Hawkins and Dave Grohl – playing together and made a pretty unique picture opportunity

CHICAGO AND CINCINNATI
MOHAWK MANIA

While the guys were enjoying a bit of a bonding session in Australia, Flea and John came up with the idea of getting Mohawks shaved for the US tour. The rest of the band pledged to do the same. Suddenly all the crew were in on the pact.

It made for a bit of an odd sight backstage. Most of them liked the new look, although lighting tech, Scott, was desperately trying to grow his out, saying he was sick of mothers pulling their frightened young kids out of his way.

All the pictures in this section are from the two gigs in Chicago and Cincinnati in August 2000.

120

John asks me whether or not he should
keep the 'tache. "What do you reckon!
Get rid mate," was my reply, and
thankfully he did

*So smart she's leading
me to ozone...*

130

AK rocks out
doing his vocal warm-up

V2001
STAFFORD AND CHELMSFORD

The only dates the band played in 2001 in the UK were the V2001 festivals as headliners in Stafford and Chelmsford. No new songs were played at either show but a few surprises were thrown in. Cover versions of 'Show of Strength' by Echo and the Bunnymen and 'Christine' by Siouxsie and the Banshees were thrown into the set to spice it up a little

133

Top: Chad relaxes with a stick of gum and a beer
Top left: Anthony perched on the edge of the stage

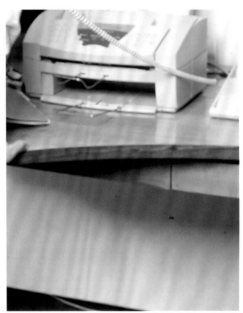

JOHN SOLO
LONDON CALLING

In January 2001, John Frusciante released his new solo album 'To Record Only Water For Ten Days'. He came to London to do press and play just one show at the 'Boarderline' – a very small, intimate venue in London. The pictures here are from the session I did with him for Kerrang, in the Metropolitan Hotel in Park Lane, London.

135

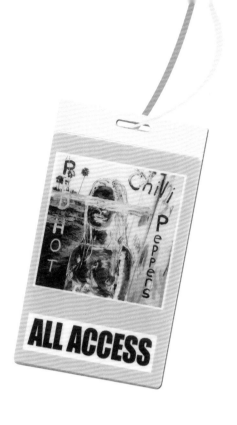

BY THE WAY
RECORDING, CHATEAU MARMONT

THE DAY ANTHONY SANG FOR ME

By the end of 2001 the band had started to record their follow-up to Californication in Ocean Studios, L.A. with Rick Rubin. In January of the following year most of the music was recorded and Anthony was preparing to record his vocals.

It was decided that Anthony would relocate from the studio and record his vocals in the more atmospheric and famous Chateau Marmont Hotel in Hollywood. Just off Sunset Blvd, it is known for the discretion and privacy afforded to its long list of famous guests. It was here where we would be based until the recording was finished.

A suite was hired on one of the upper floors with a balcony overlooking sunset strip below. The suite was divided up into the various rooms including a mini studio. The main sitting room was the focal point where Rick Rubin held court with Ethan, the recording engineer. The first main bedroom was cleared and turned into Anthony's vocal booth. He personalised the room by putting up some of his framed classic movie posters. I spent a week with AK as he did his vocals for the album, just recording everything I could, it was such a unique opportunity.

The recording session would normally start around mid-afternoon and would last until everybody was happy with how the session had gone. Anthony would arrive and start by fine-tuning his lyrics – altering previously written stuff or starting afresh with something that had inspired him that day. John Frusciante was ever present during this time, adding ideas and, of course, backing vocals to most of the tracks.

The shot of Anthony singing on the left-hand page was taken while he sang the vocals for the track 'Venice Queen' and it was a really special moment for me.

It was coming to the end of the week that I'd spent with him. I hadn't pushed it to go into the vocal room set-up, but I wanted a few shots of him in there. I asked if I could get some pictures of him singing in there – maybe we could do a dry run, not recording? Anthony immediately said no. If I was going to do it, he didn't want to fake it... he would record a track while I was in there with him. So in we went. I was told to be as quiet as I could and not to move around.

The room was delicately lit with a couple of wall-lamps. I stood in the corner by the main mic and AK came in and put on his headphones, closed his eyes and began. I took as many shots as I could while he sang the opening lines of the song...'Does it go from East to West'. Before he had finished, it struck me as sounding very different for the band. I found it quite a haunting song, brilliant, particularly the way it was being delivered on such a stripped down, personal level. It remains my favorite track the Chilis have ever done. They stretched themselves musically. Ask the crew about me and that song. My face used to light up every night they played it, as I sang along. It was an amazing experience, that I'll perhaps never get the opportunity to do again. I'm so grateful to have been given the chance.

The rest of the pictures you are about to see were taken over the five days in the hotel...

139

Home from home: John's suite with some
of his possessions dotted around the room

CALL THE COPS

I was asked to shoot the band's international press session in early May 2002 for Warner Bros. It was at the Shutters Hotel in Santa Monica where the band conducted TV, radio, and magazine interviews for five straight days to promote the new album.

My brief was to shoot individual shots in between interviews. Then on the last day, two hours was put aside for me to shoot the band in three pre-chosen locations around the hotel.

The last shots taken at the end of the session are with some LAPD Cadets who were at the hotel for a convention. As we were finishing off on the staircase they approached the guys for autographs. It was suggested that they jump in.

The other pictures in this first segment were taken at the band's rehearsal rooms in Hollywood as they worked out their set for the start of the up and coming tour dates on the By The Way tour.

154

SPECIAL REQUEST

During the second day of rehearsals in Hollywood I started shouting out a request in between songs. Every time they were deciding what to play I called for 'Knock Me Down'. It's one of my favourite songs and I hadn't heard them play it for about six years. After a while Chad yelled: "Shut the fuck up, we're not playing it and John suddenly launched into the first few chords. They all started laughing but Anthony was with Chad: "No, we're not playing THAT," he said, still laughing.

159

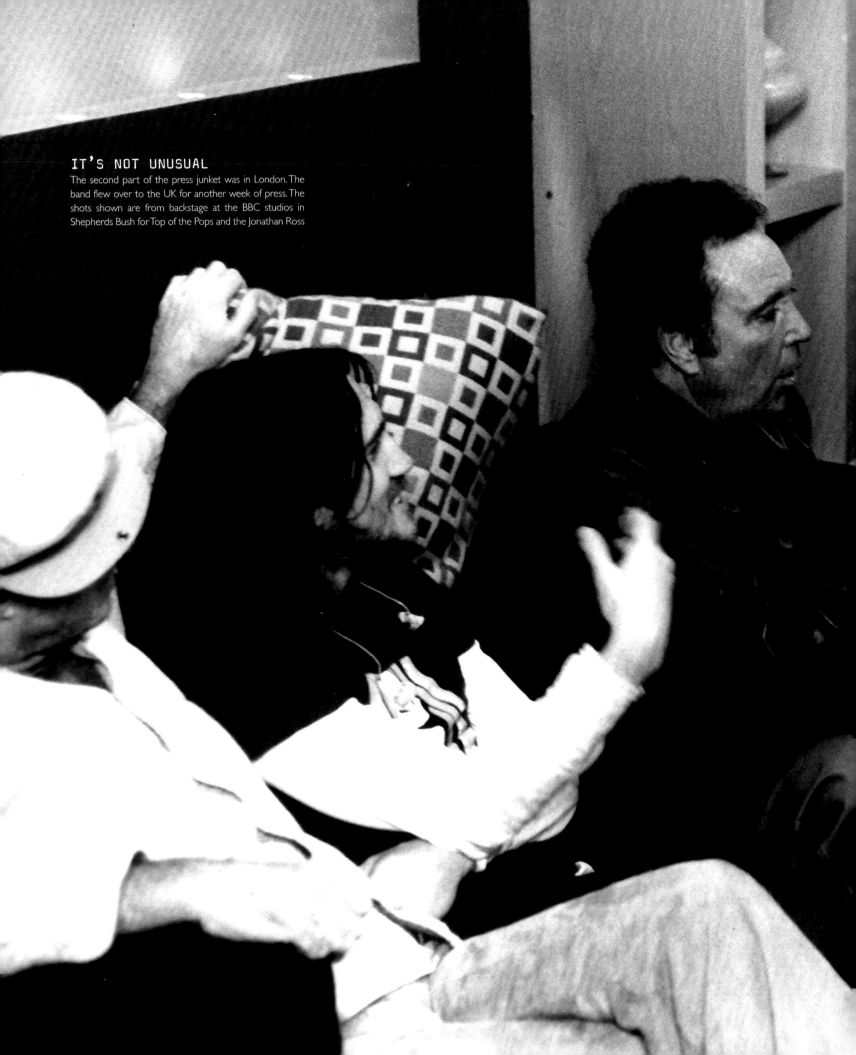

IT'S NOT UNUSUAL

The second part of the press junket was in London. The band flew over to the UK for another week of press. The shots shown are from backstage at the BBC studios in Shepherds Bush for Top of the Pops and the Jonathan Ross

The guys have a chat with Tom Jones in the green room, behind the scenes at the Jonathan Ross Show

*Performing Cabron on
the Jonathan Ross Show*

164

Anthony checks out his new tie in the hotel after going on a shopping trip along Saville Row

Filling time between
Top of the Pops and
Jonathan Ross, which
were recorded in the
same building

*AK before getting changed
for Top of the Pops*

GARAGE, LONDON
31ST MAY 2002
FAN CLUB SHOW

The Peppers played their first date of the By The Way tour as a fan club show at The Garage in Highbury, London on a very warm Friday night at the end of May.

LANSDOWNE ROAD

Two days later the band played their biggest show to date at Ireland's Lansdowne Road stadium in Dublin in front of more than 30,000 fans, which made it a very special way to start the tour.

Special guests on the night were New Order. John Frusciante, a big Joy Division fan, (which the band were previously known as before the death of their singer Ian Curtis) joined the band on stage as they played a Joy Division number. Look at the shot of John on stage with them, big smile on his face.

The band played an amazing show that night, sending the large Irish crowd home very happy.

Right: This was a funny shot. Chad took time out to pose for a picture after a song had finished. AK was ready to kick into the next track and he had a message for me and Chad which he shared with 45,000 people: "When you pair are ready we'll get on with our next track!"
Below: John playing with New Order

170

The next set of shots were taken at Wembley and the MEN Arena on the By The Way tour...

179

BY THE WAY, SOUTH AMERICA
ANTHONY ON THE BRINK. DODGING BULLETS

The band undertook a comprehensive South American tour towards the end of 2002, promoting the By The Way album and playing countries few bands visit. The show in Venezuela on October 6th was a massive event and generated a lot of media interest. It was one of the first times I had ever seen the band having to do a press conference to accommodate the interest as demand for interviews was so great.

My photo session was arranged on the roof of the hotel the band was staying in. It was a beautiful day and we had panoramic views of the whole of Caracas. There was a helicopter landing pad on the roof top and a number of steel girders hung over the edge of the roof by about eight feet all the way around.

While I was setting up my equipment Anthony did something truly amazing and incredibly risky to his own life. Raised voices caused me to look up while I was finishing loading my cameras. Anthony had walked out to the very edge of one of the four inch wide metal girders and the small group of people gathered on the roof stared

on in disbelief as he edged his way out. I grabbed my camera and shot as many pictures as I could as Anthony was perched perilously with nothing to stop him falling off the roof but the flimsy chicken wire spread from girder to girder. Finally, with Anthony safely back on the roof and the photo session over, Chad turned to me and said as we headed back down: "We may be getting old, but we're certainly not getting boring!"

Caracas was the first place I had seen the band having to use armed security. A deceptively beautiful looking city nestled in a valley, Caracas was a very dangerous place, even in the city centre in broad daylight. The band and crew were advised that if they wished to walk out of the hotel to turn right at the gates, not left. Two of the crew turned left and got mugged.

We travelled with the crew to the outdoor gig venue some miles out of the city in a mini-bus. As we were heading down the motorway and going round a bend our driver started yelling with panic. All the traffic on our side of the motorway had done a u-turn and was driving

towards us. We swerved to get out of the way and pulled over. It turned out a gun battle had started just down the road when two cars had clipped each other. After a brief argument the men involved started taking shots at each other. After making a call we had to wait five minutes for a police escort for the rest of the way.

A massive crowd gathered for the outdoor concert, the band going down a storm. On the encore they came back on stage and swapped instruments for an impromptu number. Flea played drums, Chad played lead guitar with John on bass, a great moment rarely seen. As the final note was struck Chad ran straight off stage into our waiting mini-bus ready to beat the traffic and get a head start on the trip back to Caracas, with a police escort.

We ate dinner with Chad at the hotel and reflected on a great day. Afterwards we said our goodbyes and took a taxi ride for the short journey back to our hotel. When the taxi driver went through a red light, I leaned forward and asked him if you have to stop at red lights in Caracas on a Sunday night. "Not if you want to live," he replied.

The Venezuelan flavellas
Below: Security was stepped up

*Role reversal: Chad and Flea
swap instruments*

Where are you putting those socks Flea?
Right: Chad takes in the view from his
Venezuela hotel room

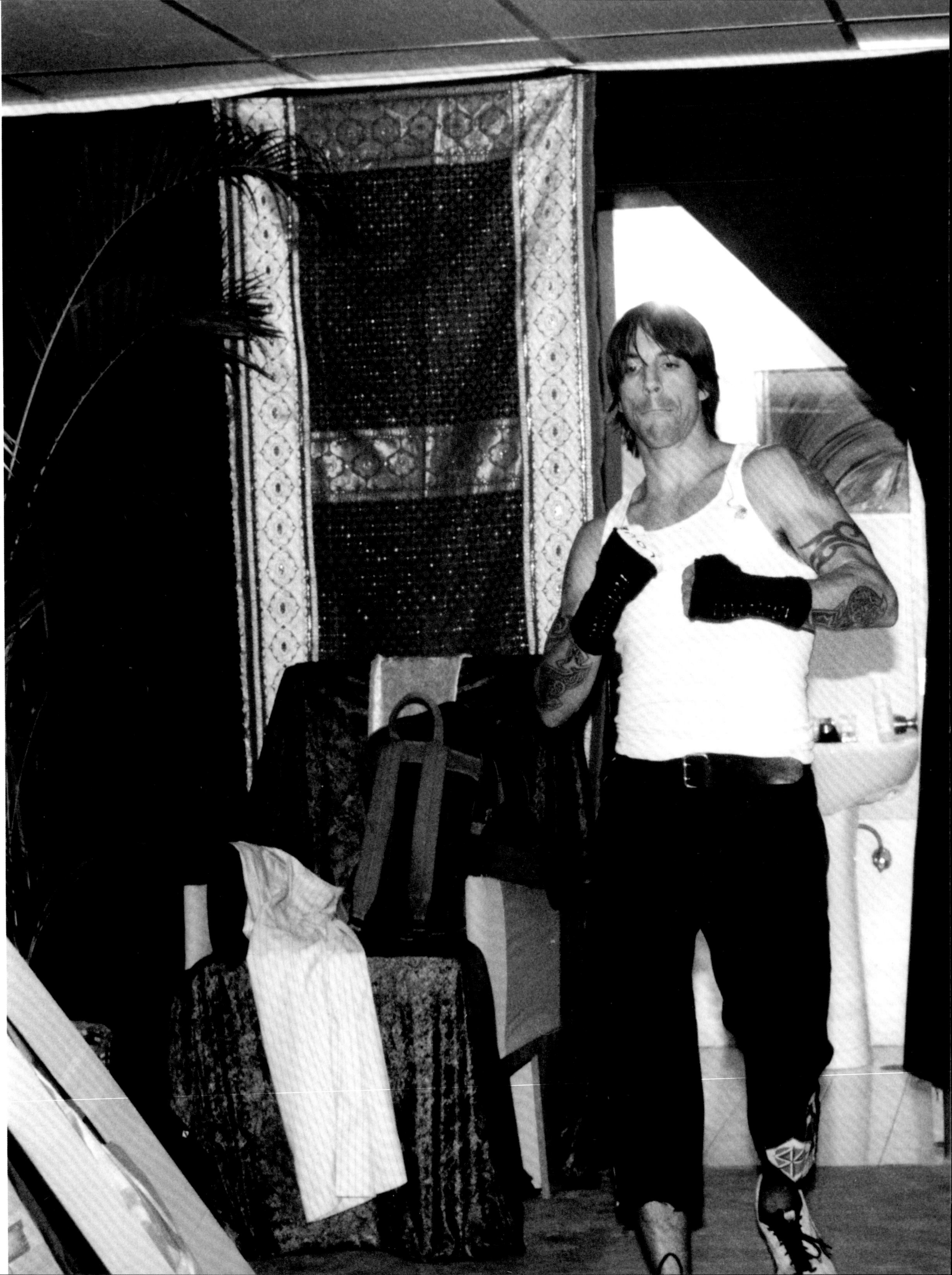

And in the Red corner...
warming-up before the gig

K-ROCK HALLOWEEN BALL
WILTERN THEATRE, LA
OCT 31ST, 2002
CHAD'S BIRTHDAY BASH

The Peppers played K-Rock's annual Halloween Ball with the Foo Fighters at the beautiful, art deco Wiltern Theatre in LA. This was a competition winners only show held by the LA radio station each year.

I was invited to Chad's 40th birthday bash at the Chateau Marmont after the gig. I covered the soundcheck and show and afterwards everybody made their way to the hotel on Sunset Boulevard for the party.

Halfway though the evening Flea made me smile when he walked up to me. "Woolliscroft, you rock," he said. "I look at you down there in the photo pit most nights and you're singing your head off to our songs with a big smile on your face." I thanked him for the compliment, it was a nice thing for him to say.

Later that night Chad asked me what I was up to the next day. I told him I was going to take pictures of a friend surfing early the next morning. "You'll make great shark bait, mate," he laughed. Nice.

That bloody comment stayed in my mind as I waded up to my waist in the Malibu surf the next day taking pictures and when I slipped and cut my leg on a rock, bleeding into the sea, I got out of the water as quickly as I could.

196

Top: Birthday boy at the soundcheck

John turns up the volume at
the V2003 festival at Stafford

Like father, like son: Anthony with his dad, Blackie, who stayed at my house for a few days with Terry Wells, the band's web designer, for the V2003 festival. We took him for a curry and we ended up having a good night at Reckless, a club in Hanley, Stoke-on-Trent. AK thanked me for looking after his dad

SLANE CASTLE
MUSIC FOR THE MASSES

One of the last European dates on the European leg of the tour was at the beautiful setting of Slane Castle, Ireland on August 23rd, 2003, a picturesque venue not too far from Dublin. Special guests were the Foo Fighters, with Queens of the Stone Age also sharing the stage.

The small country lanes couldn't cope with the traffic that led to the venue and everywhere was gridlocked. The band (except for John, who wanted to go by coach) opted to be helicoptered on to the site.

In mid-afternoon a helicopter flight was arranged to take me up over the site to capture the scale of the crowd scenes. This shot was later used on the cover of the DVD of the band's show.

The combination of performance, venue setting and lighting helped make it a truly memorable show, one of the last European dates from this album tour. The band finishing off on home soil in the US with Snoop Dogg as special guest.

John soaks up the sun at Slane Castle. The last time the guys played there was supporting U2

The guys arrive in style by helicopter, although John decided to travel on his own, arriving a bit later by coach

207

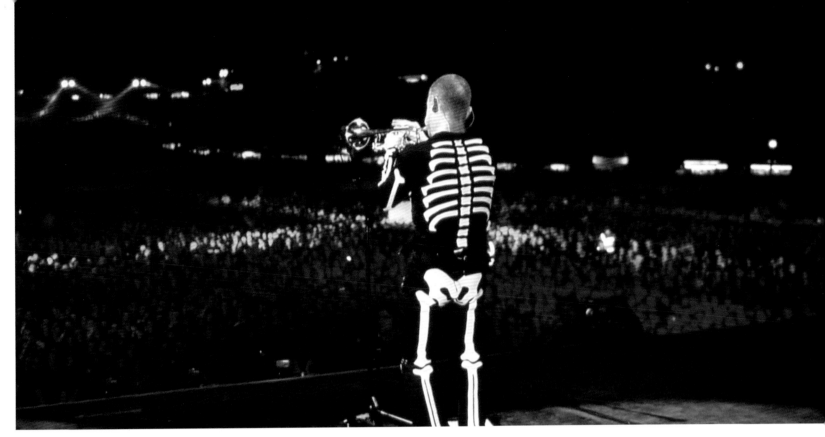

Flea blowing his own trumpet

HYDE PARK 2004
RECORD BREAKERS

At the beginning of 2004 the Peppers announced their biggest and most ambitious UK date as a solo headline act. What followed when the tickets went on sale turned out to be unprecedented, breaking all sales records. The promoters of the Hyde Park London show were in a state of panic as the show, scheduled for June 19th sold out of all 80,000 pre-sales alone. This left them with adverts placed in all national newspapers with no tickets to sell. Another date was hastily arranged on the 20th. Again this show was on its way to selling out. When they actually went on sale (with a number of new dates dotted around the country) UK phone lines went into meltdown with all dates selling out in minutes. The band were approached to play a record breaking third show in Hyde Park, again selling out in minutes, leaving the band playing to half a million people in the UK alone in just one week.

If ever there was a great deal of pressure on the band at this time, I never saw any of them showing it. The band were relaxed in a calm climate, doing ther normal pre-show rituals. There was a myriad of star guests for the London shows including Kate Moss, Elijah Wood and Jimmy Page to name but a few.

On the second Hyde Park show I was on the stage and wondered just where the hell all these people had come from. It was strange to think that in the early days this band I was involved with had played to a mere 1800 capacity at the Astoria less than half a mile away and fourteen years ago.

After the final show I spoke to Chad on the way home to congratulate him and the band on their performance. I asked why he thought the shows had sold so incredibly well? His reply: "Because of you and people like you Tony who always believed and stood by us."

I drove the rest of the way home with a smile on my face.

Old school rock fan Chad gets me to grab a picture of him with Bryan May at Hyde Park, while Rick Rubin and Kate Moss wander round backstage

214

Top left: Taking the piss: Poor Tracy, Flea's technician has to get rid of an unwanted sample after his guitarist got caught short (behind his speakers) on stage at Cardiff. Nice...

Live shot from Cardiff taken from a mixing desk chair

Walking out at Eastlands,
Manchester City stadium

The following shots were taken from the Stadium Arcadium tour at Manchester and Derby...

I thought I'd finish with a portrait of each of the guys on their own, captured in the moment, doing what they do best. Hope you enjoyed the ride. See you at the next gig...

2

EL DIABLITO

MEXICAN FIGURITAS ~ony~ *

Hello old mate.
Hope all is full of every
thing. Life is grand,
what can you say,
any thing could and
will most likely happen
today. Thank you very
much for the photos
you sent. I consider
you to be a talented and
generous man. ~Anthony~

1440 GRANT, SAN FRANCISCO, CA 94133. Tel. 141

U.S. POSTAGE
PAID
LOS ANGELES.CA
90069
OCT 28. '98
AMOUNT
$0.50
0000   00042657-05

UNITED STATES
POSTAL SERVICE

Tony Wooliscroft

Hanley Stoke on Trent
STAFFS ST1
ENGLAND.

QUANTITY POSTCARDS
Mfr. / Pub. / Wholesale / Retail / Mail Order

Catalogue
available